The Wheat-Free Dog Treat Recipe Book

Daniel Mahon

PublishAmerica
Baltimore

PublishAmerica has allowed this work to remain exactly as the author intended, verbatim, without editorial input.

Hardcover 978-1-4560-1086-7
Softcover 978-1-4560-1087-4
PUBLISHED BY PUBLISHAMERICA, LLLP
www.publishamerica.com
Baltimore

Printed in the United States of America

Your best friend shouldn't have to go without specialties because of allergies, and it's a healthy alternative for regular dogs as well!

Table of Contents

Wheat-Free & Grain-Free Dog Treats 61

NO CHARGE FOR LOVE

Wheat-Free
Dog Treats

Gluten-Free Dog Treats

1 cup gluten-free oats
1/4 cup extra virgin olive oil
1 can (or equal amount) of chicken broth
1 cup instant potato flakes
1 beaten egg
1/3 cup powdered milk

Mix oats, oil and milk. Add chicken broth and mix again. Let it sit for five minutes (so the oats can soak up some liquid) and then add the potatoes and egg. and mix it all together. Roll with rolling pin to a thickness of 1/4 inch. Cut into bars, squares or use a cookie cutter. Bake at 250(f) for 90 minutes, or until completely dried and crunchy.

Tuna Treats

2 6-oz. cans tuna in water, do not drain
2 eggs
1 to 1 1/2 cups rice flour
parmesan cheese

Mash tuna and water in a bowl with a fork to get clumps out, then liquefy in blender or food processor. Add extra drops of water if needed to liquefy completely. Pour into bowl and add flour; consistency should be like cake mix. Spread into greased or sprayed pan; I find that a round pizza pan or square cake pan is perfect. Sprinkle with LOTS of parmesan cheese. Bake at 350 degrees for 15 minutes; edges will pull away and texture will be like putty. Use a pizza cutter and slice into teeny squares. These freeze great, and the dogs love them.

Banana Treats

3 cups oatmeal
1 1/4 cups rice flour
2 eggs
1/4 cup oil
1/2 cup honey
1/2 cup milk
2 mashed bananas

Blend liquid ingredients, eggs and mashed bananas, making sure to mix well. Add flour and oatmeal. Mixture will be similar to cake mix. Spread into a well-greased pizza pan and bake at 325 degrees for about 25 minutes. Cut into tiny squares or strips using a pizza cutter. Keep refrigerated; store unused in freezer.

Turkey Treats

1 lb. ground turkey
1 cup oatmeal
1 egg
1/2 cup parmesan

Mix all ingredients together using hands and pat into a greased loaf pan. Bake at 350 degrees for 30-35 minutes. Cool *thoroughly*, then cut into thick strips (these do not hold together when slicing into small squares); freeze unused portions and keep the portions you're using refrigerated. Has the consistency of meatloaf.

Salmon Treats

15oz can of Salmon or Jack Mackerel
some flour
2 tsp of salt
1 tsp of baking powder

Mix together fish, plus ALL liquid from can, salt & baking powder, add enough flour for texture. Spread out on cookie sheet. Score into sections (easier to break apart when done). Bake at 350 degrees for about 30 mins. or crust is golden. Store in container in frig or freezer for longer periods of time

Dog Cookies

3 cups rice flour
2 small cans dog food
1 egg
1 1/2 to 2 cups liquid (I make sure it isn't to dry or to wet so you may have to make your own judgment as to how much liquid to use. I use broth as the liquid).

Preheat oven to 375 degrees. Stir together all ingredients and drop by spoonful on greased cookie sheet. Bake for 12-14 minutes.

After they are cooled down I cut them into small pieces with kitchen shears then put them in freezer bags and store in the refrigerator.

Sunflower Cookies

2 cups Rice Flour
2/3 cup Yellow Cornmeal
1/2 cup Shelled Sunflower Seeds (can substitute pumpkin seeds)
2 Tbsp Corn Oil
1/2 cup beef or chicken broth
2 eggs mixed with 1/4 cup lowfat milk

Glaze:

Beat 1 egg. Lightly brush on cookie before baking

Preheat Oven to 350 degrees. In a large bowl, mix dry ingredients and seeds together. Add oil, broth, and egg mixture. Your dough should be firm. Let sit for 15-20 minutes. On a lightly floured surface, roll out dough ¼ inch thick. Cut into shapes and brush with glaze. Bake for 25-35 minutes until golden brown. Cool. Store cookies in airtight container.

Vegetarian Dog Treats

1 medium yam or sweet potato
1/2 Cup Peanut Butter
1/2 Cup cooking liquid from yam
1 Cup Rice flour (brown or white)
1 Cup Oat flour (use gluten free oats for gluten free dog treats)
2 tsp. baking powder

Cut yam or sweet potato into 1/2 inch pieces. Simmer in a small pan, in enough water to cover, until soft. Reserve cooking liquid and set aside. In large bowl, mash the yam. Add 1/2 C liquid back to the yam with the peanut butter. Mix the Baking powder together with the flour. Add to the Yam mixture mixing thoroughly.

It should all come together in a dough, pliable but not sticky. If too sticky to roll out, add more flour, if too dry, add more liquid—just a bit at a time—and work together with your hands until it is the right texture to roll out. A good texture is like slightly dry cookie dough.

Roll out on a lightly flour dusted surface. about 1/4 inch thick. Cut into small shapes with a cookie cutter, (bone and people shapes are fun). Place on cookie sheets. Bake at 375 for 30 minutes +/- or until medium golden brown. (The larger the cookie the longer the time.) Cookies will crisp up as they cool. Makes about 4 dozen small dog treats.

Beefy Potato Treats

2 cups potato flour
3 cups rye flour
4 tbsp fresh parsley (chopped)
1/2 cup vegetable oil
2 cups beef stock

Blend the potato and rye flour together. Mix in the parsley and vegetable oil. Slowly add the beef stock until a stiff dough is formed. Place the dough on a floured counter or surface and roll about 1/2 think and cut into shapes with cookie cutters (or make flattened balls). Place on a non-greased cookie sheet and bake at 350F for about 30 to 35 minutes or until crisp.

Veggie Rice Treats

1/2 cup powdered milk
1 cup vegetable stock
4 cups rice flour
2 cups shredded carrots

Blend all of the ingredients together. Drop tablespoons of the dough onto a cookie sheet. Bake at 350F for 30 to 40 minutes or until done. Let cool on the cookie sheet.

Liver Brownies

1/2 cup rice flour
2- eggs (medium)
1 1/2 lbs liver (beef)

Puree all of the ingredients together in a food processor. Pour into a greased 9 inch square pan. Bake at 350F for 30 minutes or until the mix springs back when touched. Cut into shapes and store in the refrigerator.

Parmesan Crisps

6 oz Parmesan cheese (grated)
3/4 cup Fresh Parsley (chopped)
1 cup Cornmeal
1/2 Chicken stock

Blend all of the ingredients together. Drop tablespoons of the mix onto a greased cookie sheet. Bake at 375F for 10 minutes or until the cheese melts and the cookies become crisp.

Liver Snaps

2 cups rice flour
1/2 cup peanut butter
2- eggs (medium)
1/2 cup water
1/2 lb liver (cooked and diced)

Blend the flour, peanut butter, eggs, and water together. Add the diced liver and more flour to make the dough stiff. Place dough on a floured counter and roll about about 1 inch and cut into shaped with cookie cutters (or make flattened balls) and place on an non-greased cookie sheet. Bake at 350F. for 25 to 30 minutes or until the treats are brown and crisp.

Ginger Spiced Treats

2 tbsp ginger (finely shredded)
4 cups rice flour
2 tsp- cinnamon (ground)
1 cup water
1/2 cup molasses

Blend the ginger, flour, and cinnamon together. Slowly add water and molasses to the flour mix to form the dough. Place on floured counter and roll out about 1 inch think and cut into shapes with cookie cutters (or make flattened balls). Bake at 350F for about 25 to 30 minutes or until brown and crisp.

Betsy's Best Biscuits

2 cups rice flour
1 cup oatmeal
2 tbsp olive oil
1 cup beef stock

Blend rice flour and oatmeal together. Add the oil and slowly stir in the beef stock in order to form a stiff dough. Place the dough on a floured surface and roll out about 1/2 inch thick and cut in to shapes with cookie cutters (or make flattened balls). Place on a non-greased cookie sheet and bake at 375F for 25 minutes or until golden brown.

Sam's Rewards

4 cups rice flour
1/2 cup powdered milk
2 tbsp red wine vinegar
1 cup beef stock
1/2 cup vegetable oil

Place the flour and powdered milk in a mixing bowl. Add the red wine vinegar, beef stock, and vegetable oil, and blend until you make a stiff dough. Place the dough on a floured counter and roll out about 1 inch and cut into shapes with cookie cutters (or make flattened balls). Pierce each treat with a fork and bake on a non-greased cookie sheet at 375F for 25 minutes or until firm.

Breath Busters

3 tbsp vegetable oil
1- egg (medium)
1/2 cup fresh mint (chopped)
1/2 cup fresh parsley (chopped)
2/3 cup milk
2 cups brown rice flour

Combine the oil, egg, mint, parsley, and milk and whisk together. Blend in the flour slowly and beat until you form a stiff dough. Place the dough on a floured counter and roll out about 1/2 inch and cut into shapes with cookie cutters (or make flattened balls). Place on a non-greased cookie sheet and bake at 350F for 25 to 35 minutes or until golden brown.

Peanut Butter Pupcakes

2 cups rice flour
2 tbsp salt free veggie broth powder
2 tsp baking powder
1/3 cup vegetable oil
1 egg, beaten
1 cup vegetable stock or rice milk
1/2 cup peanut butter

Preheat oven to 350. Combine flour, baking powder. Add remaining ingredients. Grease muffin tins. Spoon batter into tins, about 2/3 full. Bake 15-25 minutes. When cool frost with peanut butter.

Carrot Cookies

2 cups rice flour
1/2 cup nutritional yeast
6 tbsp oil
1 egg, beaten
1 tsp molasses
1 cup mashed cooked carrots

In a large bowl, combine flour and yeast. In another bowl, mix oil, egg, molasses, and carrots. Add wet ingredients to dry and stir. Form dough into little balls. Place them on a greased cookie sheet. Smoosh each ball with a fork or cookie stamp. Bake at 325 till crunchy.

Dog-gone Good Corn Bread

1 cup cornmeal
1 cup rice flour
4 tsp baking powder
1 cup rice milk
1/2 cup corn oil

Combine cornmeal, flour, and baking powder. In a separate bowl or measuring cup combine rice milk and oil. Beat until smooth. Pour into a greased 8" square pan and bake at 425 degrees for 15-20 minutes.

Peanut Butter 'Nilla Biscuits

1 1/2 cups water
1/2 cup oil
3 tbsp peanut butter
2 tsp vanilla
2 cups rice flour
1/2 cup cornmeal
1/2 cup oats

In a large bowl, combine flour, cornmeal, and oats. Stir in oil, peanut butter, vanilla, and water. Knead till smooth, adding more flour or water as needed. Roll out on a lightly floured surface. Cut with cookie cutters. Bake on a greased cookie sheet at 400 degrees for 20 minutes.

Peanut Butter Bow-wow Bites

2 cups rice flour
1 cup peanut butter
1 egg, beaten
1/4 cup vegetable oil
3/4 cup water

Preheat oven to 350 degrees. Combine flour, peanut butter, egg, oil and water and mix thoroughly. When it becomes too stiff to stir, knead the dough till smooth, adding a tablespoon of water, if needed. Roll to 1/4 inch thickness. Cut into desired shapes. Bake for 30-35 minutes, being careful not to over cook.

Cheese N' Veggies Treats

1/2 cup low fat, cheddar cheese, grated
1/4 cup butter
1 small jar, pureed carrots (baby food)
1 small jar, pureed mixed vegetables (baby food)
1 cup rice flour (extra might be needed)
1/4 tsp. celery flakes
1/4 cup chicken broth

Melt butter and cheese in a saucepan and remove from heat. Add celery flakes, baby foods and flour. Stir until well blended. Add enough broth to form a ball of dough. You may need a bit more or less that the amount noted in the recipe. Chill dough in the freezer for 1 hour or so. Ensure that the dough is covered with kitchen wrap so it doesn't dry out. Roll dough on a floured board to 1/4" thickness. If it's too sticky, add a bit more flour and try again. Place on a non stick cookie sheet and bake in a 350 degree oven for 30 minutes, or until golden brown. Cool before storing in a sealed container

Grainy Crunches

1/2 cup barley flour
1 cup rye flour
1/3 cup chicken broth
2 Tbs. Safflower oil
1/2 Tsp. parsley flakes

Mix flours. Add broth and oil. Mix well. Roll dough onto a board and cut into shapes or strips. Place on a non-greased cookie sheet and bake at 350 degrees until golden.

Meat the Dog

1 pound ground beef
1 egg, beaten
1 cup quick cook rolled oats
3 cups barley flour
1 cup beef broth
1/2 Tsp. Kelp

Combine meat and egg in a food processor . Mix until well blended. Combine oats and flour in a large bowl and begin to mix the meat in slowly. Work it until it's blended well. Add kelp and mix again. Add broth to produce a dough that's somewhat sticky. Knead on a floured surface and add flour if needed. Roll dough to 1/4 inch thickness. Cut into shapes or simply use a knife to shape squares or triangles. Place treats on a non stick cookie sheet and bake for approx. 1 hour at 350 degrees F. The treats should be well done and will harden further as they cool.

These do not need to be refrigerated and they won't last long enough to worry about it.

Apple Treats

2 cups rice flour
2 cups rye flour
1/3 cup cornmeal
1 egg, beaten
1 tbsp safflower oil
1 apple (grated)
1/2 tsp cinnamon
1 - 1 1/2 cups, cold water

Combine all ingredients in a bowl- except the apple and water. Grate apple into mixture and add part of the water. Turn out on a floured surface and incorporate more water if the dough is too stiff while kneading for 2 minutes or more. Roll out to a thickness of 1/4" Use a knife to score the dough vertically and then horizontally so you have squares.

Don't cut right through the dough. Place on a nonstick cookie sheet and bake at 325 degrees F for 1 hour or until golden and you have a firm sheet of baked product. Let cool. Break off into pieces.

Baby Food Dog Treats

3 Jars Baby Food—beef & carrots /chicken
1/4 Cup Cream Of Rice
1/4 cup Dry milk powder

Combine ingredients in bowl and mix well. Roll into small balls and place on well-greased cookie sheet. Flatten slightly with a fork.

Bake in preheated 350°F oven for 15 minutes until brown.

Cool on wire racks and STORE IN REFRIGERATOR.
Also freezes well. If frozen, microwave for 3-4 minutes on Medium High.

Cheese Bone Dog Treats

2 cups Unsifted rice flour
1 1/4 cups Shredded cheddar cheese
1/2 cup Vegetable oil
4 1/2 tbsp Water (up to 5 tbsp.)

Preheat oven to 400°F. Make a cardboard pattern of a dog bone, 4 inches long or use a dog-bone cookie cutter. Combine flour, cheese, and vegetable oil in container of food processor. Cover, whirl until mixture is consistency of coarse meal. With machine running, slowly add water until mixture forms a ball. Divide dough into 12 equal pieces. Roll out each piece to 1/2" thickness. Cut out bones. Transfer to non-greased cookie sheet. Bake in preheated hot oven for 10 to 15 minutes or until bottom of cookies are lightly browned. Carefully transfer bones to wire rack to cool completely. Refrigerate in airtight container.

Oatmeal Dog Treats

3 cups rye flour
3 cups Uncooked oatmeal
6 tbsp Margarine
1/4 cup Molasses
1 cup Evaporated milk
1 cup Water

Mix together the first 3 ingredients. Then thoroughly mix in the last 3 ingredients. Dough will be stiff. Chill for a half hour. Roll rounded teaspoonfuls into balls. Flatten, place on greased cookie sheet, and bake for 1 hour at 300°F.

Glazed Beagle Biscuits

1/3 cup oil
1 cup boiling water flavored with meat or chicken drippings
2 cups rolled oats
3/4 cup cornmeal
1/2 cup milk
1 cup grated cheese
1 egg beaten
1 cup rye flour
2 cups rice flour

Topping:

1 cup beef broth
3 tbsp oil

Add bouillon and oil to boiling water then add oats. Let mixture stand for a few minutes. Stir in the cornmeal, milk, cheese, and egg. Slowly stir in the flours. Knead on a lightly floured surface until the dough is smooth and no longer sticky. Roll out to about 1/4 inch thick and cut into bone shapes. Place on a greased baking sheet. Spoon topping over biscuits. Turn them over and repeat with other side. Bake at 325 degrees for 45 minutes or until lightly browned on bottom. Turn off the oven and leave biscuits in until cool.

Tuna Biscuits

1 cup yellow cornmeal or 1/14 cup corn flour
1 cup oatmeal
1/4 tsp. baking powder
1 small can tuna in oil, undrained
1/3 cup water

Grind oatmeal in processor to make a coarse flour. Set aside in small bowl. In food processor, whirl tuna with the oil, and water then add all the rest of ingredients. Pulse till mixture forms a ball, Pulse to knead for 2-3 minutes. Knead on floured surface till it forms a soft ball of dough. Roll out to a 1/8"-1/4" thickness. Cut into shapes. Bake on lightly greased cookie sheet, at 350 for 20-25 minutes. Cool completely.

Pumpkin Treats

1 1/2 cups rice flour
1/2 cup pumpkin, canned
1 tbsp brown sugar
1/2 tsp ground cinnamon
1/2 tsp ground nutmeg
4 tbsp Crisco
1 whole egg
1/2 cup buttermilk

Preheat oven to 400 degrees. Combine flour, cinnamon and nutmeg and cut in shortening. Beat egg with milk and pumpkin and combine with flour, mixing well. Stir until soft dough forms. Drop by tablespoons onto non-greased cookie sheet and bake for 12 to 15 minutes. Let cool and serve.

Munchy Crunchy Meat Treats

1/2 cup non-fat powdered milk
1 egg, beaten
1 1/2 cups rice flour
1 tsp. honey
1/2 cup water
5 tsp. chicken or beef broth
1 jar baby food meat (any flavor)

Combine all ingredients well. Form into a ball. Roll dough out on a floured surface. Cut out desired shapes. Bake in a 350 degree oven for 25-30 minutes. Let cool. The treats should be hard and crunchy.

Tempting Treats

2 1/3. cup rice flour
1/4 cup olive oil
1/4 cup applesauce
1/2 cup grated cheese (like parmesan)
1 large egg
1/4 cup non-fat powdered milk

Combine all ingredients in a large bowl; mix well; Roll the dough out to size of a cookie sheet; Pat the dough onto a lightly greased cookie sheet, bringing it to the edges.

Using a sharp knife or a pizza cutter, cut desired sizes into dough (just score through). If you're using as training treats, cut them into small pieces; Sprinkle a little extra cheese if desired on dough for flavor. Bake in a 350 degree oven about 15 minutes until golden brown. Turn off the oven and let cool for a few hours; They will keep hardening the longer you leave them. Break them apart; store tightly covered or in the freezer

Bulldog Brownies

1/2 cup shortening
3 Tbsp. honey
4 eggs, beaten
1 tsp. vanilla
1 cup rice flour
1/4 cup carob powder
1/2 tsp. baking powder

Cream shortening and honey together thoroughly. Add remaining ingredients. Beat well. Bake in a greased cookie sheet (10x15") for 25 minutes at 350 degrees. Cool completely.

Frosting:

12 ounces non-fat cream cheese
2 tsp. honey

Blend together. Spread frosting over cool brownies. Cut into 3 inch or 1 1/2 inch squares.

Thanksgiving Treats

2 lbs. ground turkey
2 eggs, beaten
2 cups cooked rice
8 oz. peas
3 carrots, diced
1 apple, diced

Preheat oven to 375 degrees. In mixing bowl, combine all ingredients. Mix well by hand. On baking sheet, form into the shape of a large dog bone. Bake at 375 degrees for 45 minutes. Let cool and serve.

Low Fat Chicken & Bean Treats

3 1/2 cups rice flour
1 cup Cornmeal
1/4 cup Skim milk
3/4 cup Chicken stock
1/2 cup Green bean puree (green bean baby food works well)

Blend the rice flour and cornmeal together and set aside. Whisk together the skim milk, chicken stock, and green bean puree. Slowly add the flour mix to the bean mix until you have formed a stiff dough. Place the dough on a floured surface and roll out 1 inch thick and cut into shapes with cookie cutters (or make flattened balls) and place them on a non-greased cookie sheet. Bake at 350F for 35 minutes or until the cookies are crisp.

Good Boy Surprise

2 cups Rye flour
1/2 cup Rice flour
1/4 cup Cornmeal
1/2 cup Vegetable oil
1/2 cup Water

Blend rye flour, rice flour, and cornmeal, together. Whisk together the oil and water. Slowly add the flour mix to the water and oil to form a stiff dough. Add more water if needed to make the dough more workable. Place the dough on a floured surface and roll out about 1/2 inch thick and cut into shapes with cookie cutters (or make flattened balls) and place on a non-greased cookie sheet. Bake at 375F for 35 minutes or until the treats are crisp.

Cran-Apple Treats

2 cups Rice flour
1 cup Oatmeal
3/4 cup Milk
1/2 cup Fresh apples (minced)
1/4 cup Cranberries (minced)

Mix together the rice flour and the oatmeal. Stir the milk into the flour mixture. Add the minced apples and cranberries. Place the dough on a floured counter and roll it out about 1/2 inch think and cut into shapes with the cookie cutters (or make flattened balls). Place the cut outs, or balls, on a non-greased cookie sheet. Bake at 250F for 25 to 35 minutes or until the treats are golden brown and firm.

Natural Dog Treats
(flavor them yourself)

2 cups of rice flour
1/2 cup of oatmeal
1/4 of a cup of vegetable oil
1 egg, beaten
1 cup of water

Preheat the oven at 350°F. Mix all ingredients in a large bowl, except the water. To flavor the biscuits, add a flavoring ingredient to the water. Chicken stock or Beef stock. The batter is pretty heavy, it's normal! Roll the batter about 3/4 of an inch thick on a flat surface, using a bit of flour under so it does not stick. Cut the batter using dog biscuit cookie cutters or a knife. Place the
cookies on a baking sheet. Cook for 20 minutes, then turn the cookies over and cook for another 20 minutes. Then, turn the oven off and let the cookies dry out for an hour or two.

Apple Cinnamon Bites

4 cups rice flour
1/2 cup cornmeal
1 egg
2 tbsp vegetable oil
1 small apple (grated)
1 tsp cinnamon
1 1/3 cups of water

In a bowl combine all ingredients except the apple and water. Grate apple into mixture and add water. Mix until it starts forming together. Turn out on a lightly floured surface. Knead well. Roll out to a thickness of 1/4 - inch to 1/2 - inch. Take a straight edge and score the dough horizontally then vertically to make a grid of 3/4 squares. Be careful not to score the dough that it completely cuts through the dough. Place on a baking sheet that has been sprayed with a nonstick spray. Bake at 325 degrees F for 1 hour.

Peanut Brindle Treats

5 cups rice flour
1 tbsp cinnamon
1 tsp baking powder
1 tsp baking soda
1 cup peanuts (chop)

In a bowl, mix all ingredient except chopped peanuts together thoroughly.
Set aside.

1 egg
1/4 cup honey
1/4 cup peanut butter
1 small apple
1/2 cup vegetable oil
2 1/2 tsp vanilla
1 1/2 cup water

In a food processor, add the above ingredients and blend together. When mixture is thoroughly blended, add to the bowl of dry ingredients. Combine and turn out on a lightly floured surface. Place a piece of plastic wrap on top of dough then roll out dough to 1/4 - inch thickness. Remove the plastic wrap and score dough into 4 by 3-inch rectangles. Spritz the top of the rectangles with water and sprinkle chopped peanuts over them. Press the chopped peanuts in to the dough with the palm of your hand. Bake at 325 degrees F for 50 to 60 minutes.

New Puppy Treats

1 stick butter
1 tsp Brown sugar
1/4 tsp Salt
1 cup Coarse ground corn meal
2 cup Rice flour
1 cup Nonfat dry milk powder
2 Eggs
Juice from 2 cans of tuna

Preheat oven to 350 degrees. Mix all ingredients. Sprinkle a clean surface with extra corn meal or flour, and roll out dough to about 1/4 inch thickness. Cut into shapes with cookie cutters or into squares or bars. Bake on a non-greased cookie sheet for 20 to 25 minutes or until brown. Some seemed underdone while others were overdone. Next time, try baking at 325 for a longer time.

Carob Molasses Dog Treats

6 cups white rice flour
1/8 cup peanut oil
1/8 cup margarine, preferably safflower oil type
1 tbsp brown sugar
2 oz carob, chips melted
1 cup water
1/4 cup molasses
1/2 cup non-fat dry powdered milk

Preheat oven to 300 degrees. Grease or spray cookie sheets
Mix dry ingredients in a large bowl. Add remaining ingredients and
mix until blended. Dough will be stiff. Chill. Roll dough on a greased
cookie pan and cut into shapes 1/2 inch thick. Bake for 1 hour.

Snickerdoodles

1/2 cup vegetable oil
1/2 cup shortening
1 cup honey
2 eggs
3 3/4 cups white rice flour
2 tsp cream of tartar
1 tsp baking soda
1/2 cup cornmeal
2 tsp cinnamon

Mix vegetable oil, shortening, honey with eggs. Beat well. Add flour, soda and cream of tartar. Knead dough until mixed well. Shape dough by rounded teaspoons into balls. Mix the cornmeal and cinnamon together in a bowl and roll balls in mixture. Place 2 inches apart on a greased cookie sheet . Press the balls down with a fork. Bake for 8-10 minutes at 400F. Cool on a rack. Store in airtight container.

Oatmeal Cookie Treats

2 cups rice
2 packages Reg. Flavor oatmeal (mixed w/milk)
1/4 cup molasses
1 cup carrots
1/3 cup spinach
1 1/4 cup rice flour
1/2 tbsp brown gravy mix
4 tbsp applesauce
1/2 tbsp vegetable oil

Preheat oven to 350 degrees Stir Ingredients, but adding flour gradually. Drop on cookie sheet using tsp. Bake 15-20 minutes or until golden brown.

Meat & Sweet Potato Dog Treats

1 Lb ground meat (lamb, beef, chicken, turkey)
1 large sweet potato (cooked and mashed)
1 large egg
5 tbsp. large flake rolled oats

Preheat oven to 350 degrees.
Combine all ingredients in a bowl, mixing up very well. Lightly grease a cookie sheet with olive oil. (very slightly)
Dump ingredients on cookie sheet and spread evenly and flatly to the sides of pan. This should be about 1/4 to 1/2 inch thick. Bake for one hour at 350 degrees.
Remove pan from oven and use your cookie cutter at this time, if you want. If you don't have a cookie cutter, just score the 'cookie dough' with a knife or pizza cutter, into squares.
Put back into the oven and bake for another hour at 250 degrees.
This will dry these healthy dog treats out. Keep an eye on your oven.

The time could be more or less, depending on how hot your oven runs. These dog treats should be fairly dry and a little crispy, but not burned.

Peanut Butter & Bacon Treats

2 pieces bacon, thick cut, cooked and crumbled
1/8 cup bacon grease
2 cups rice flour
1/4 cup ground flax
1/4 cup bran
2 tsp baking powder
1/2 cup peanut butter
1 egg, lightly beaten
3/4 cup water

Preheat oven to 325° F. Cook bacon until crispy. Drain on a paper towel. Pour the bacon grease into a glass measuring cup. In a large bowl, whisk together the flour, ground flax, bran, and baking powder. Crumble the bacon, once cooled, and stir into the flour mixture. In a microwave safe bowl, warm the peanut butter. Approximately 30 seconds. In a medium bowl, lightly beat the egg. Then pour in the peanut butter, water, and bacon grease. Use a fork to whisk together the wet ingredients until completely combined. Make a well in the dry ingredients, and pour in the peanut butter mixture. Stir until combined. Knead lightly in the bowl with your hands. Lay down one large sheet of parchment paper, roll your dough onto it, then lay another piece of parchment on top. Roll out to 1/2 inch thickness. Lightly spray a baking sheet with non-stick cooking spray. Cut shapes out of the dough and place on your prepared baking sheet. Gather the extra dough, knead into a ball, and repeat the process of rolling and cutting until there is no more dough. Bake for 15 minutes. Turn off the oven and leave them there to cool for 2 hours or overnight. Storing - These treats will stay fresh in the refrigerator for two weeks. Freezer: up to 6 months

Mean Lean Treats

(For Dogs on a Diet)

1/2 cup shredded cheddar cheese, low or fat free
3 1/2 cups rice flour
1/2 cup green beans, mashed
1 cup beef broth, reduced sodium, plus 1/4 cup for glaze
1/4 cup milk, low or fat free
1 tbsp olive oil

Additional Flour for Rolling

Preheat oven to 350° F
Gently toss the cheddar cheese and the flour in a large bowl. Set aside.
In a small bowl, mash the green beans. Stir in the broth, milk, and olive
oil to the green bean mixture. Make a well in the center of the cheese
flour. Pour in the green bean mixture and mix thoroughly. Knead the
dough in the bowl until combined. Fold out onto a floured surface and
continue to knead using extra flour. Knead until you have a firm dough.
Cut out shapes. Place the cut outs on a baking sheet that has been lightly
sprayed with non-stick cooking spray. Pour 1/4 cup of beef broth into
a small bowl. Using a pastry brush, lightly brush the broth onto the cut
outs. Bake for 30 minutes.
Treats will keep fresh in the refrigerator for 3 weeks. Freezer: 6
months.

Wheat-Free & Grain-Free Dog Treats

Easy Treats

1/2 cup instant potatoes
1 tsp. grated ginger
1/2 tsp. cinnamon
2 Tbsp. molasses
2 Tbsp. extra virgin olive oil

Mix all wet ingredients. Mix all dry ingredients. Mix it all together. Knead the dough until well blended. Roll out to 1/4 inch thick. Cut into bars, squares or use a cookie cutter. Bake at 300(f) for 45 minutes, then turn off the oven and let the cookies sit in there until the oven is cool. They should be completely dried and crunchy.

Meaty Treats

1 pound of ground meat (cooked, use beef, chicken, fish or lamb)
1 large sweet potato (cooked and mashed)
1 large egg
1/2 cup water
Oil to coat the pan with

Preheat your oven to 350(f) degrees Combine egg, sweet potato and water in large bowl. Allow to sit for 10 minutes. Add meat and mix well. Spread on lightly oiled baking sheet. Cut into bars or squares Bake for 30 minutes and remove the pan from oven. Use a spatula to turn them over, then bake them again for 20 more minutes. Remove them from the oven and cool them on a wire rack. Serve when cool. Yield is approximately 30 - 45 squares or bars.

Misty's Veggie Bars

1 large sweet potato, diced in 1/2 inch chunks
4 cups of water
3 carrots, cut in coins
3 - 4 cups instant potato flakes
Oil to grease the pan

Preheat the oven to 375F degrees. Chop the vegetables and put them into a pot. Add the water. Turn the heat on high under a covered pot and cook the vegetables until very soft when pierced with a fork. Take the pot off the heat and remove the lid. Mash the vegetables until they're all smashed good. Add the instant potato flakes and stir. It should be kind of stiff, it shouldn't move when the spoon is pulled out. If it does, add more potato flakes and mix them in. Line a baking sheet with foil and then oil the foil. Dump the mixture onto the baking sheet. Spread it out evenly all over the pan, filling out the corners. Make sure it's evenly spread, so there aren't thick and thin spots. Take a knife and cut the mixture into squares or bars, depending on the size of your dog and the size of treat desired. Bake in the oven for 25 minutes, then turn down the temperature to 250F degrees and leave the pan in for another two hours. Don't open the door to see how they're doing in the last two hours, it's necessary for them to cool down slowly. After two hours remove the pan from the oven and turn the bars over with a spatula and then put them back in the oven for an hour more. At the end of the hour, turn off the oven and leave the treats in until completely cooled. They should be hard with softer centers and the corners may have browned during the high temperature period. That's perfectly normal and it's been found that dogs don't mind one bit. Cool completely before serving. Store the treats in an air-tight container in the refrigerator.

Liver Bites

1 lb. chicken liver
1 cup graham cracker crumbs
3 tablespoons molasses or honey
1/4 cup parsley

Place all ingredients in the bowl of food processor. Process until smooth. Pour into a microwaveable container, approximately 8" square or round. Microwave on high until a toothpick inserted in the center comes out clean. This takes 7 minutes in my microwave, but your watts may vary. When cooked, turn out of pan immediately, allow the bottom to dry since it will be damp from condensation, and cut into squares while still warm.

Spread bits on a foil-lined cookie sheet and bake at 200° for 1.5 hours.

Freeze or refrigerate.

Canine Muffins

1 small jar of baby applesauce
2 carrots
2 Tbsp honey
2 ¾ cup water
1/4 tsp vanilla
1 egg

Shred the carrots with hand shredder or food processor. In a bowl, mix all wet ingredients together and add the applesauce. Mix thoroughly.

4 cups rice flour
1 Tbsp baking powder
1 Tbsp nutmeg/pumpkin pie spice

Combine dry ingredients.

Add wet ingredients to dry and mix thoroughly, scraping the sides and bottom of the bowl to be sure none of the dry mixture is left. Grease a muffin tin with non-stick spray. (Paper liners stick to the muffins so just use a greased muffin tin) Using an ice cream scoop, fill each cup 3/4 full. Bake at 350° for approximately 1 hour. Makes about 2 dozen Canine Muffins.

Turkey "dogs"

ground turkey meat (any amount)
low sodium breadcrumbs (potato bread (wheat free))
parmesan cheese
parsley flakes

In a large mixing bowl, add 1 tsp (per lb of meat) of parsley and 1 tbsp (per lb of meat) of parmesan cheese to the meat. Stir in breadcrumbs until the mixture is somewhat dry. You should be able to form small balls and roll sausage shaped treats between your hands without having the mixture stick to your hands (too moist) or crumble apart (too dry). Place on jelly roll pan lined with aluminum foil. Bake at 350 until the sausages are lightly browned on the outside and fully cooked on the inside. Remove to absorbent paper towels and blot the sausages to remove excess grease.

Store cooled sausages in ziploc bags in the freezer.

For training treats, cut sausages into raisin sized pieces.

Fish Bars

2/3 cup cooked fish fillet—boned and chopped
3/4 cup instant potato flakes
3 tsp steamed carrots, chopped
3 tsp cooked green beans

In a bowl, combine all the ingredients. Spread on a greased baking sheet and bake at 375(f) for 25 minutes, then cut into bars while it's still hot. Move to cooling rack and completely cool before serving.

Keep refrigerated or put them in the freezer. Dogs love these when they're frozen solid, plus it cleans their teeth like crunchy foods do.

Savory Cheese Treats

1 cup instant potato flakes
3/4 cup shredded cheddar cheese
5 tablespoons grated parmesan cheese
1/4 cup plain yogurt or sour cream

Preheat the oven to 350 degrees. Combine cheeses and yogurt. Add instant potatoes. If needed, add a small amount of water to create a nice dough. Knead dough into a ball and roll to 1/4 inch. Cut into one inch sized pieces and place on greased cookie sheet. Bake for 25 minutes.

Puppy Cookies

2 jars (3 1/2 oz.) strained beef baby food
1/4 cup dry milk

Mix ingredients. Roll into small balls. Put onto greased cookie sheet.
Flatten with fork. Bake at 350 degrees until brown.

Liver and Potato Dog Treats

1 lb. liver
1 egg
1 1/4 cup potato flakes
beef or chicken broth

Preheat oven to 400° F. Cut liver in to 1" pieces. The size does not need to be accurate since you will be pureeing it. However, the smaller size helps aid the process. Place ingredients, liver and potato flakes, into a food processor. Pulse ingredients. Be ready to add the broth as needed to make the mixture spreadable into the pan. The consistency will be very thick. Pour into a greased 13 x 9 pan. Bake for 25 minutes. Let cool on a wire rack for 5 minutes. Use a knife to loosen, then invert pan and empty onto a wire rack.
Let it cool completely before cutting.
Storage: 2-3 weeks in refrigerator, in a dog treat jar.

The following treats have yogurt.
Please give to your dog in moderation.
Too much could make them sick.
Suggest no more than 2 per day.

Puppy Pops

1 Quart fruit juice
1 banana, mashed
1/2 cup yogurt

Mix ingredients together thoroughly, then freeze. This can be eaten by people too.

Frozen Peanut Butter Yogurt Treats

1-32oz. container of vanilla yogurt
1 cup of peanut butter

Put the peanut butter in a microwave safe dish and microwave until melted. Mix the yogurt and the melted peanut butter in a bowl. Pour mixture into cupcake papers and freeze. Great for those really hot days!!

Frosty Paw Treats

32 oz. Vanilla yogurt
1 mashed banana or one large jar of baby fruit
2 Tbsp. Peanut butter
2 Tbsp. Honey

Blend all together and freeze in either 3 oz. Paper cusp or ice cube trays. Microwave just a few seconds before serving.

Note: Baby meat can be substituted instead of the fruit and peanut butter.

Easy Dog Ice Cream

16 oz non-fat plain yogurt
1/4 cup creamy peanut butter
1 ripe banana
1/8 cup peanut butter chips
1/8 cup carob chips

Mix all well in mixer on medium-high speed until well blended. Pour into small containers and freeze. 1/2 cup plastic disposable containers work great.

NO CHARGE FOR LOVE

A farmer had some puppies he needed to sell. He painted a sign advertising the 4 pups. And set about nailing it to a post on the edge of his yard. As he was driving the last nail into the post, he felt a tug on his overalls. He looked down into the eyes of a little boy. "Mister," he said, "I want to buy one of your puppies." "Well," said the farmer, as he rubbed the sweat off the back of his neck, "These puppies come from fine parents and cost a good deal of money." The boy dropped his head for a moment. Then reaching deep into his pocket, he pulled out a handful of change and held it up to the farmer. "I've got thirty-nine cents. Is that enough to take a look?" "Sure," said the farmer, and with that he let out a whistle."Here, Dolly!" he called. Out from the doghouse and down the ramp ran Dolly followed by four little balls of fur. The little boy pressed his face against the chain link fence. His eyes danced with delight. As the dogs made their way to the fence, the little boy noticed something else stirring inside the doghouse. Slowly another little ball appeared, this one noticeably smaller. Down the ramp it slid. Then in a somewhat awkward manner, the little pup began hobbling toward the others, doing its best to catch up…"I want that one," the little boy said, pointing to the runt. The farmer knelt down at the boy's side and said, "Son, you don't want that puppy. He will never be able to run and play with you like these other dogs would." With that the little boy stepped back from the fence, reached down, and began rolling up one leg of his trousers. In doing so he revealed a steel brace running down both sides of his leg attaching itself to a specially made shoe. Looking back up at the farmer, he said, "You see sir, I don't run too well myself, and he will need someone who understands." With tears in his eyes, the farmer reached down and picked up the little pup.

Holding it carefully he handed it to the little boy. "How much?" asked the little boy. "No charge," answered the farmer, "There's no charge for love."

~Author Unknown~

LaVergne, TN USA
09 January 2011
211722LV00010B/52/P

Table Of Contents

Introduction

I want to thank you and congratulate you for purchasing the book, "The Best Of Beautiful Netherlands for Tourists: The Ultimate Guide for Netherlands Top Sites, Restaurants, Shopping, and Beaches for Tourists!".

This book contains proven steps and strategies on how to enjoy a vacation in The Netherlands.

The Netherlands is known across the world as a progressive country. Many tourists go to this country for different reasons. This book shares information about the various tourist destinations, shopping sites, restaurants, and beaches in different parts of this country. A chapter is also dedicated to the arts and culture of The Netherlands so that tourists will understand what kind of country they will be visiting.

Thanks again for purchasing this book, I hope you enjoy it!

Chapter 1: Tourism in The Netherlands

The Netherlands has always been a haven for tourists from around the world. In fact, there is a yearly increase in the number of tourists who visit the country. World renowned for its Delft pottery, windmills, and tulips, the Netherlands is also famous for its free-spirited capital, Amsterdam. Found in the northwestern part of Europe, the small country boasts of the Frisian Islands, canals and bridges, farmlands, beautiful villages, and highly populated cities.

Amsterdam is the most popular city in the country because of the party scene, red light district, the Anne Frank House, art museums, medieval architecture, and scenic canals. Tourists can start from this city and take advantage of different day tours to check out different places around the country. The Hague is known as the Dutch royal family's home as well as the seat of government. Zaanse Schans and Volendam are popular for their customs, windmills, costumes, and traditional Dutch houses. The town of Lisse is a popular tourist spot during spring for its flowers. The town of Alkmaar is a great place to visit for its cheese market.

The Netherlands is known for its cuisine which basically consists of vegetables and meat, Dutch apple pie, smoked sausage, and fried meatballs. Tourists can also opt to dine in different international restaurants around the country. In terms of transportation needs, tourists can go around by buses and trains. Because of the good roads and flat land, they can also go cycling.

For tourists going to The Netherlands, they have to ensure that their passports have enough unused pages and are valid for at least 3 months after departure from the country. Tourists may require securing a visa before traveling to the country. However, US citizens are not required to have a visa if they only plan to stay in the country for a maximum of 3 months.

Chapter 2: Tourism in Various Regions of the Netherlands

In 2011, tourists flocked to the northern part of The Netherlands. An estimated 6 million guests visited the region. The southern part, on the other hand, had 1.4 million tourists. Belgians, Britons, and Germans were the top visitors of The Netherlands. The country is famous for its 7 World Heritage Sites. Because it is a small country, tourists can travel from north to south in just one hour.

North Holland

Amsterdam is located in the northern part of the country. Around 4.3 million foreigners visited the city in 2011. Famous museums like Rijkmuseum, Ann Frank House, and the Van Gogh Museum are top tourist spots. The city's canal ring is considered a World Heritage Site. Drug tourists flock to Amsterdam because cannabis consumption and prostitution are legal in The Netherlands. On the northern part of the capital, tourists visit the Zaanse Schans for its windmills, and Marken and Volendam for their old fishing villages. Alkmaar is famous for its old center and cheese market. The castle of Muideeslot is found on the southeast side of Amsterdam. The town of Naarden has a well preserved star fort while Haarlem is noted for its old city center and historical legacy. Zandvoort, a seaside resort near Haarlem is famous for its car racing circuit.

South Holland

In 2013, around 849,000 tourists visited the Keukenhof, which is noted as the largest flower garden in the world. Keukenhof is only open to the public during the spring season. Kinderdijk is famous for its 19 windmills and is recognized as a World Heritage Site. On the other hand, The Hague is often visited for its government buildings like the Ridderzaal and the Binnenhof. The Mauritshuis is an art museum which is also frequented by tourists in the area. Tourists troop to Scheveningen because of its beach. A miniature park is found in Madurodam.

Found in the northern part of The Hague, Leiden is popular for its national museums like the Rijkmuseum van Oudheden and Naturalis. Considered as the world's oldest botanical garden, the Hortud Botanicus Leiden is also a popular tourist site. Katwijk and Noordwijk are popular resorts by the sea. Delft is located on the southern part of The Hague and is popular for its old center and pottery. William the Silent, touted as the founder of modern Netherlands, has a museum in his name in Delft.

Other Regions In The Netherlands

The city of Utrecht has the tallest church tower in the country. It also houses the Netherlands Railway Museum and the Musical Clock Museum. Tourists can also visit the Slot Zuylen Castle and the Kasteel de Haar. Efteling is near Kaatsheuvel and is considered one of the oldest theme park around the world. It is also the country's entertainment park. Effenaar is famous as a music venue in Eindhoven. The Slot Loevenstein is a castle located in the province of Gelderland. The country's oldest city, Nijmegen, is popular because of the International Four Day March during the month of July. Another popular site in Gelderland is the Netherlands Open Air Museum. Mudflat hiking is possible from Friesland mainland to the West Frisian Islands during low tide. Middleburg boasts of various seaside resorts in the province of Zeeland.

Chapter 3: Top Tourist Sites In The Netherlands

Some parts of The Netherlands are reclaimed from the sea. Most tourists only visit Amsterdam. However, the country still has a lot to offer aside from its capital city. Cycling is perfect in most areas because the landscape is flat and crisscrossed with canals. Guests can visit historic town centers and other tourist sites around The Netherlands. The long coastline is peppered with sandy beaches and protective dunes. Flower gardens are popular during springtime.

The Delta Project is a series of storm surge barriers, dikes, locks, sluices, and dams which were built from 1950 to 1997 in South Holland and Zeeland. The American Society of Civil Engineers included the site to the Seven Wonders of the Modern World. Maastricht Vrijthof is a popular city square in South Holland. It showcases the Saint Jan's Cathedral and Saint Servatius Church. Huge festivals are also held in the city of Maastricht all year round.

Found in Amsterdam, the Rijksmuseum is the coubtry's most prestigious and largest art and history museum. Works of Rembrandt and Vermeer are showcased there. Kinderdijk, on the other hand, has the most number of Dutch windmills in one site. The Hoge Veluwe National Park is the biggest continuous nature reserve with woodlands, sand dunes, and heath lands. Inside the park is the Kroller-Muller Museum which has a huge collection of Vincent van Gogh's paintings.

To promote the country's flower industry, The Netherlands has Keukenhog Gardens which is recognized as the largest flower garden in the world. Yearly, about 7 million flower bulbs like tulips, daffodils, and hyacinths are planted in the park. The garden is open from late March up to the middle of

May. The Delft City Hall is a tourist attraction because of its Renaissance building. Designed by Hendrick de Keyser, it has undergone a lot of changes and was restored to its original Renaissance appearance in the 20th century.

The West Frisian Islands is a series of islands found in the North Sea. Licensed guides help the guests tour the islands by walking on mudflat. Known as Rembrandt's birthplace, Leiden boasts of beautiful canals. Popular for its oldest university, its old center is the 2nd largest 17th-century town center in the country. Finally, Amsterdam's canals form concentric belts which consist of 3 major canals like Keizersgracht, Prinsengracht, and Herengracht.

Gouda is popular among day trippers. It is famous for its cheese, clay pipes, candles, and syrup waffles. Tourists can take the highway and railway to go to this city. Rotterdam, on the other hand, is considered the most modern city in The Netherlands. Tourists go to this city for its carnivals and festivals during the summer season. The Museum Boijmans Van Beuningen has a collection of works of masters like Rembrandt, Bosch, Van Gogh, and Dali. The university city of Groningen has 2 colleges. Its Groninger Museum is the most modern and innovative in the country.

Unofficially dubbed as the flower city, Haarlem hosts the Annual Bloemencorso Parade. Located near the Spaarne River, it has medieval structures which tourists can experience. Museums and architecture are stunning and shopping is always enjoyable in Haarlem. The Teylers Museum is the country's oldest museum and features science, arts, and natural history exhibits. Utrecht, on the other hand, has a rich Middle Age history. The University of Utrecht is the largest university in the country. The Gothic Cathedral of Saint Martin, the Museum Speelklok, the

Rietveld Schroder House, and the Dom Tower are also popular tourist spots.

The city of Maastricht is famous for its Vestigingswerkens, Saint Jan's Cathedral, and Saint Servatius Church. Furthermore, Helpoort and St. Pietersberg Caves are also worth visiting. Popular for its Royal Picture Gallery Mauritshuis and the Gemeentemuseum Den Haag, The Hague offers a glimpse of Dutch Royalty. Tourists enjoy the North Sea during the warm months in Scheveningen. They can enjoy the international art galleries, cozy shops, and luxury stores. The Hague is home to the seat of government, known as the Binnenhof. Madurodam is the city's miniature city.

The city of Delft is progressive. Tourists can enjoy a day trip to visit the Prinsenhof, a museum which showcases a lot of intriguing works. Leiden, a beautiful city, is a popular tourist spot because of its tree-lined, scenic canals as well as its lush parks, wooden bridges, and old windmills. Visitors can enjoy a boat ride along its canals. Lastly, Amsterdam is famous for its unique coffee shops, pubs, galleries, and shops. Its popular museums are favorites among museum hoppers.

Details on Various Tourist Sites

The following are some of more popular tourist sites in Netherlands. This may not be extensive but it provides you with some of the best places to see in the country. Some of the attractions mentioned on this list are quite popular, which makes them very easy to find. There are a lot of interesting things to see and learn in this country.

Anne Frank House

The Anne Frank House opened its doors to the public on May 3, 1960. This is one of the really popular attractions in North Holland. If you have read and appreciate The Diary of Anne Frank, then you will enjoy the things you will find here. The place itself is a historical monument. Today, her old war time shelter has been converted into a biographical museum. It is the 3rd most visited museums in the Netherlands today. You can find this historic museum at Prinsengracht 263-267, 1016 GV Amsterdam, Netherlands.

Keukenhof

This marvelous garden is the second biggest flower garden in the entire world. It opened in 1950 and it has also been called as the Garden of Europe. It's actually one of the most visited places in the province of South Holland. The name Keukenhof actually translates to "kitchen garden." This massive garden covers a total land area of 79 acres and they grow more about 7 million bulbs. Visitors can marvel at the sight as they walk amongst the tulips. You can find Keukenhof garden at Stationsweg 166A, 2161 AM Lisse, Netherlands.

Artis Zoo

The full name of this zoo is Natura Artis Magistra. It is centrally located at the very heart of Amsterdam. This is actually one of the oldest zoos in all of Europe. Additional features of this zoo are its planetarium and aquarium (built in 1882). The zoo also houses a lot of historic buildings, which includes a library that was established in 1867. You can find Artis Zoo at Plantage Kerklaan 38-40, 1018 CZ Amsterdam, Netherlands. The zoo is usually open from 9 am to 5 pm. Children 2 years old and below get free entrance.

Entry fees range from € 16.50 to 19.95 for children and adults.

Vondelpark

Vondelpark is the most popular and the largest public urban park in Amsterdam. It was designed following English landscaping designs. The park is centrally located in the city and is near some of the places of interest in the metropolis. The park welcomes around 10 million visitors a year. You can enjoy the lovely surroundings or be part of the audience in one of the many open air concerts – all for free. You can find the park at southern end of Leidseplein.

Stedelijk

If you enjoy a lot of modern art then you will like what you will find in The Stedelijk Museum. Their collections feature some of the best contemporary pieces of art and design. The building itself follows after renaissance revival architecture. A huge portion of their collection dates back to the 20th to the 21st century. They also have in their collection some of the works of popular artists such as Vincent van Gogh, Jackson Pollock, Wassily Kandinsky, and Marlene Dumas among others. You can find Stedelijk at Museumplein 10, 1071 DJ Amsterdam, Netherlands.

Rembrandt House Museum

Rembrandt House Museum is both a historic house as well as a museum dedicated to famed painter and artist Rembrandt. Rembrandt Harmenszoon van Rijn lived in this very house from 1639 to 1656. It was here where he produced his greatest works. Here you will find the artist's paintings and sketches. Part of the collection also includes works from his contemporaries. Artists and fans of the arts will find the place as some sort of hallowed ground filled with rich inspiration. You can find the Rembrandt House Museum at Jodenbreestraat 4, 1011 NK Amsterdam, Netherlands.

Heineken Experience

Heineken Experience is one of the really old breweries in Amsterdam. Today, the place serves as the visitor's center of one of the biggest breweries in the country – Heineken Beer. The original brewery was established in 1867. It produced some of the best beers and drinks until 1988 when a newer and more modern brewing facility was erected. It was reopened in 1991, no longer as a brewery but a visitor's center where tourists can appreciate the old beer brewing art. You can find the Heineken Experience is at Stadhouderskade 78, 1072 AE Amsterdam, Netherlands.

Ons' Lieve Heer op Solder - Museum in Amsterdam, Netherlands

The name of this museum translates to "Our Lord in the Attic." The building itself is intriguing. The building served as a clandestine church where Catholics held their religious services in secret in the 17th century. The church itself was built on upper floors. Today, this fascinating building serves as a museum. The museum was inaugurated in 1888. Thousands of visitors and foreign tourists visit the Ons' Lieve Heer op Solder each year. You can find the museum at Oudezijds Voorburgwal 40, 1012 GE Amsterdam, Netherlands.

The National Maritime Museum

The National Maritime Museum is one of the popular museums in North Holland. The building used to be a naval storehouse. As the name suggests the theme of this museum is maritime history. The building itself was constructed way back in 1656 but the museum was moved here in 1973. If you're interested in the old ways of sailing and ancient shipping, then this museum will provide you with a lot of striking details. You'll find the museum at Kattenburgerplein 1, 1018 KK Amsterdam, Netherlands.

Verzetsmuseum (Dutch Resistance Museum)

Verzetsmuseum is dubbed as the number one historical museum in the country. It is located in North Holland. The museum houses war time artifacts from World War II. Here in this museum, visitors will find vivid retellings on how the Dutch resisted German occupation from 1940 to 1945. You'll find the Dutch Resistance Museum at Plantage Kerklaan 61A, 1018 CX Amsterdam, Netherlands.

Madurodam

This tourist attraction is actually a miniature park. It is located in The Hague in South Holland. It opened its doors to the public in July 2, 1952. You can call it as a city within a city where miniature replicas of the popular landmarks in Holland are replicated and given life. The mini city bustles with a lot of life with little cars driving more than 22,000 kilometers each year. Its miniature railway is an astounding network that stretches up to 4 kilometers in length. You'll find Madurodam at George Maduroplein 1, 2584 RZ Den Haag, Netherlands.

Jordaan

Jordaan is probably one of the most popular and most scenic neighborhoods in Amsterdam. Note that this is actually an upscale neighborhood, so expect some of the things here to be quite expensive. Students and lovers of modern art will find the many museums here as a huge boon. Here you'll find specialty shops and rows of restaurants serving the local cuisine. Jordaan is located at Tweede Goudsbloemdwarsstraat 19, 1015 JX Amsterdam, Netherlands.

Euromast

Euromast is an observation tower in Rotterdam. Visitors may think of it as an odd structure jutting out of the ground. However, as you get closer, you'll find the design to be quite ingenious. The way the tower was built, its center of gravity is actually located beneath the ground. Its observation deck is situated 315 feet up in the air. It also has a restaurant on the same deck. The tower with the antennae on top has a total height of 606 feet. You can find Euromast at Parkhaven 20, 3016 GM Rotterdam, Netherlands.

Begijnhof

This site is the oldest of Amsterdam's inner courts. Visitors will find an entire neighborhood of historic buildings. It is unclear when the Begijnhof was established. However, the name of the place suggests that it was once owned by a community of women that lived a semi-monastic lifestyle. It is also said that its courtyard was probably constructed in 1389, but the details aren't clear. Nowadays, it is the site of the English Reformed Church. You can find Begijnhof at Begijnhof 30, Amsterdam, Netherlands.

Royal Palace of Amsterdam

The Royal Palace of Amsterdam first opened its doors to the public in 1665. It is one of the three palaces in the country that is under direct management of the monarchy. It is one of the lasting heritages the country has of the Dutch Golden Age. The palace was erected as the town hall of the city. It was an enormous undertaking that took around 17 years to complete. The interiors are lavish, as should be expected of any residence for royalty. The total cost of the construction cost around 8.5 million Francs. Royal Palace of Amsterdam is located at Dam, Amsterdam, Netherlands.

Museum Boijmans Van Beuningen

Museumpark 18, 3015 CX Rotterdam, Netherlands is one of the oldest art museums in Rotterdam. It was officially opened in 1849. Its collections include the works of renowned artists such as Salvador Dalí, Vincent van Gogh, Claude Monet, and Rembrandt. It is one of the most visited museums in the Netherlands. Many of the most noted works housed here include The Little Tower of Babel, Glorification of Mary, The Face of War, and Impressions of Africa. Museum Boijmans Van Beuningen is located at Museumpark 18, 3015 CX Rotterdam, Netherlands.

Dom Tower of Utrecht

If you're interested in the unique architecture in the Netherlands, then you'll notice that part of the style is an emphasis on the height of a structure. The churches here exemplify that notion. And the tallest church tower ever built here is the one at the Dom Tower of Utrecht. This tower has become the symbol the city of Utrecht. It follows suit with Gothic architecture. It stands at a massive height of 112.5 meters. Dom Tower of Utrecht is located at Domplein 9, 3512 JC Utrecht, Netherlands.

Hermitage Amsterdam

The Hermitage Amsterdam is a branch of the Hermitage Museum in Russia. It is one of the leading attractions in North Holland. Back in 1682 when the building was completed, the place served as a retirement home. Elderly folks lived here until the 90's when it was determined that the facilities were no longer fit for housing retired senior citizens. Today, the Hermitage Amsterdam holds art exhibits and public lectures. Hermitage Amsterdam is located at Amstel 51, 1018 EJ Amsterdam, Netherlands.

Kröller-Müller Museum

Have you ever seen a garden full of sculptures? That is exactly what will greet you when you walk into the grounds of the Kröller-Müller Museum. This is one of the many popular art museums in the Netherlands. It opened back in 1938. One of the most interesting collections in this museum is its wide array of pieces made by no other than Vincent Van Gogh. In fact, it holds the second largest collection of the artist's works. The largest collection is in the Van Gogh Museum. Kröller-Müller Museum can be found at Houtkampweg 6, 6731 AW Otterlo, Netherlands.

Van Gogh Museum

The Van Gogh Museum holds the largest collection of the works of Vincent Van Gogh. It is one of the most visited museums in the Museum Square. The Van Gogh Museum opened in June 3, 1973. The museum also holds a considerable collection of the works of Van Gogh's contemporaries which includes artists such as

The museum has sculptures by and paintings by Henri de Toulouse-Lautrec, Auguste Rodin, Paul Signac, Jules Dalou, Émile Bernard, Maurice Denis, Georges Seurat, Kees van Dongen, Odilon Redon, Paul Gauguin, Claude Monet, and Édouard Manet. The Van Gogh Museum is located at Paulus Potterstraat 7, Amsterdam, Netherlands.

Museum of Bags and Purses

Museum of Bags and Purses is one of the most unique museums in the world. Imagine a museum dedicated to historic luggage. The collections you will find here include suitcases, purses, and handbags – all of them are historic or notorious for one reason or another. The collection includes thousands of items, some of which date all the way back to the 16th century. The Museum of Bags and Purses is located at Herengracht 573, 1017 CD Amsterdam, Netherlands.

Chapter 4: Top Restaurants In The Netherlands

The Dutch cuisine is a sophisticated mix of exotic and local ingredients using traditional French culinary techniques. Some restaurants use Zeeland lamb, pigeon, local livestock, langoustine, lobsters, and mussels.

Located near the southwest part of The Netherlands, near the Belgian border, Oud Sluis is a restaurant and guesthouse in the town of Sluis and famous for its various oyster preparations. It also offers home-grown and seasonal produce. Restaurant De Librije is inside a library of a 15th-century monastery with old world charm and high ceilings. It offers tasting menus with exotic and classic ingredients. Cod stomach, rabbit kidneys, acid bomb, and -20 degrees Celsius-cooked egg yolk.

Ron Gastrobar is in Amsterdam and offers an eclectic menu in surprising textures and tastes. Ciel Bleu is famous for its cuisine as well as the view it offers to Amsterdam diners. The menu includes truffled macaroni, lobster in farmhouse butter, Siberian sturgeon caviar, and King crab. De Lindenhof, on the other hand, is a restaurant in a farmhouse with lush garden. It offers Belgian and Dutch cuisine. It is located in a village known as the "Venice of the Netherlands", Giethoorn. It can only be accessed through boats because cars are not allowed in the village.

Located at the north of Haarkem, De Bokkedoorns is a French restaurant offering pigeon in red beet sauce, cod sashimi with creme fraiche, and blini. 't Brouwerskolkje is also in Haarlem and offers a menu using a blend of molecular and traditional techniques. Because it only has 6 tables, tourists must make reservations. Boreas has a great garden terrace and modern ambiance in a 20th-century villa in Heeze. Its menu is a mix of innovation and tradition.

Located near the coast of Zeeland and the beautiful villages of Zierikzee, Veere, Middleburg, and Yerseke, Inter Scaldes is both a manor and a restaurant. The menu includes Zeeland lamb, bass, mussels, lobster, and oyster. Da Vinci is in Maasbracht and offers simple menu which changes every 5 weeks. Restaurant Beluga offers impeccable service. The menu is rich in local seasonal ingredients. The restaurant is located in Plein.

Parkheuvel is located in Rotterdam and is popular for its seafood. Da Zwethheul, on the other hand, is famous for its tartar of scallops, goose liver and truffle, and jelly of lobster. The restaurant is near the Schie River in Schipluiden. Just outside of Maastricht, in a small village, is De Leuf. The restaurant is known for 4 and 6 course menus. Guests can stay overnight in this picturesque farm. Finally, De Leest is famous for its wine and seafood. It is situated outside of Apeldorn.

Chapter 5: Highly Recommended Restaurants for First Timers

La Oliva Restaurant

La Oliva is situated in one of the nicer areas in Amsterdam. Many customers revere the pintxos and the fritatas. But of course, this restaurant has more to offer. A lot of items on the menu are from the Spanish cuisine but you'll find a lot of burgers, salads, and other items for heavy lunches and dinners. The atmosphere is great even though the restaurant can get really busy at times. The background music also helps set customers on a relaxed eating mood. Another thing that really needs mentioning is the fact that they have a pretty extensive wine list.

La Oliva Restaurant is open from 12 noon to 10 pm. They're open until 11 pm on Thursdays. The restaurant is at Egelantiersstraat 122-124, 1015PR Amsterdam, The Netherlands (Jordaan).

HanTing Restaurant

There must be something wonderfully cooking at HanTing Restaurant. It is one of the favorite restaurants (and perhaps the best) in The Hague – and that's coming from both local and foreign tourists who have been there. Guests have raved about the food, service, and atmosphere at HanTing. First impressions would have you guessing that they only serve Chinese Food here but you'll be pleasantly surprised after perusing the menu. It's a fusion of French and Oriental cuisine!

HanTing Restaurant is at Prinsestraat 33, 2513 CA Den Haag, Netherlands. They're open Tuesdays to Sundays from 5:30 pm all the way to 10:30 pm.

Beddington's

Beddington's is named after the owner of the restaurant. The restaurant opened for business back in 1983 and it has been a big hit since then. The menu makes a unique Dutch twist to many French, English and Asian favorites. Where else can you find wasabe on mouthwatering seared tuna? Are you ready for a potato mash infused with a one of a kind soy sauce concoction? Their creations are no less than creative and the atmosphere fits business type folks as well as gastronomic diners as well.

The restaurant is open from 6 pm to 10 pm. Beddington's Restaurant is at Utrechtsedwarsstraat 141, 1017 WE Amsterdam, The Netherlands (Stadsdeel Zuid).

Lieverd Restaurant

Lieverd is arguably the best restaurant in Scheveningen. Some people will contest that but you really have to try what they have to offer before you protest. They serve a mix of Dutch, Mediterranean, German, French, and European cuisines. Each week they feature a different menu that highlights a particular ingredient. That means your options, no matter which cuisine you choose, will have that featured ingredient in it. Some have said that it that sounds a lot like The Iron Chef come to life. There's really no need to mention that the guys preparing the food there are highly creative. The only downside to Lieverd is that the place can be a bit pricey at times. It's up to you to judge if the food and service is worth it's weight in gold.

Lieverd Restaurant is at Stevinstraat 170, 2587 ET Scheveningen, The Hague, Netherlands. They're open from Tuesdays to Sundays from 5:00 pm to 11:00 pm.

De Kas

The name of this restaurant literally translates to "green house." Well, that's pretty much what you'll find in the décor. The other thing about this place is the fact that they grow their own food. If not, then it wouldn't be much of a green house, wouldn't it? The food is served with a bit of flair but you can easily distinguish the European style cooking.

De Kas is at Kamerlingh Onneslaan 3, 1097 DE Amsterdam, The Netherlands. They're open from Mondays to Fridays from 12 noon to 2 pm. On Saturdays they're open from 6:30 pm to 10 pm.

Restaurant Mazie

Restaurant Mazie is one of those restaurants that can easily make it to the top 5 list in The Hague. They serve authentic European cuisine in 3 or 5 courses. Another plus is the generous pouring of wine. Their wine selection is good but there's still a big chance that they will pick things up. Not a few customers who wrote reviews about Mazie comment that the restaurant definitely deserves its first Michelin star.

Restaurant Mazie is at Maziestraat 10, 2514 The Hague, The Netherlands (Kortenbos). They're open from 6:00 to 10:00 pm on Tuesdays, 12:00 pm to 10:00 pm on Wednesdays to Fridays, and 6:00 pm to 10:00 pm on Saturdays.

Restaurant Greetje

Greetje is a restaurant that bullheadedly sticks to its roots. They serve the local Dutch cuisine with a twist. Now, some of the locals may think that a commercial dining place should serve something more, the geniuses working the kitchens here think otherwise. In fact, the way they recreated the country's traditional dishes is something truly remarkable. It goes beyond just making Dutch stamppot the way your grandma should make it – it goes beyond your expectations. The restaurant staff is superbly attentive and they definitely know what's on the menu – every detail.

Restaurant Greetje is located at Peperstraat 23, 1011 TJ Amsterdam, The Netherlands (Binnenstad). They're usually open from 6 to 10 in the evening but they usually stay up late until 11 pm during Saturdays.

Irawaddy Restaurant

Irawaddy serves authentic Thai cuisine and due to their unique choice of meals, they have become quite an easy favorite for many customers. Tourists in particular are usually curious and often leave the restaurant as truly satisfied customers. The ambiance good, quaint, but good – it may need some improvement to appeal more to a generally European crowd. But the food is where it hits the spot. You may not always appreciate the décor but the pad thai will leave you breathless. You can find Irawaddy Restaurant at Spui 202, The Hague, Netherlands.

Vis aan de Schelde

If you love seafood and you don't mind going off the beaten track then you will love what they have in store at Vis aan de Schelde. The place is family friendly and relaxed. It's the type of place where you want to bring the entire family or perhaps your fiancée's parents. The wine list is quite extensive and the staff can even suggest which ones go best with the food you ordered.

They're open Mondays to Fridays at noon until 2:30 pm and from 5:30 pm to 11 in the evening. During weekends, they only open from 5:30 pm to 11 pm. Vis aan de Schelde is at Scheldeplein 4, 1078 GR Amsterdam, Netherlands.

HofTrammm Restaurant

A meal at the HofTrammm is no less than a truly moving experience. Some even say that this restaurant should be on the top 5 restaurant list on The Hague. This restaurant serves authentic European cuisine. They serve a fixed menu but they also accommodate vegetarians. The drinks are also pretty good and the staff is quite generous when they pour your wine. Note that dining options here are upon reservatio only. You can't just walk in as you please. The food and service can be a bit pricey at certain times of the year but that's money well spent. HofTrammm is at Rond de Grote Kerk, The Hague, The Netherlands.

Razmataz

If you're hungry for something Mediterranean or French then this is the go to restaurant. Just ask the locals. Don't forget the day's specials listed on the blackboard. The restaurant attracts a diverse crowd but many customers are usually young and upbeat. The staff is friendly but service tends to get a bit slow at times, perhaps due to the crowd that comes and goes – heavy traffic is always very hard to manage.

Razmataz is open from Mondays to Thursdays from 8.30 am to 1 am. On Saturdays they're open from 9 am to 3 am. And on Sundays they're open from 9 am to 1 am. You can find the restaurant at Hugo de Grootplein 7, 1052 KV Amsterdam, Netherlands.

De Eetkamer van Scheveningen Restaurant

There's really nothing wrong with being the second best even if we're dealing with rankings of the best restaurants in The Hague. This restaurant serves a mix of French fusion, which is to die for. The only downside is that the menu isn't as extensive as you hoped it would be.

The De Eetkamer van Scheveningen Restaurant is located at Marcelisstraat 255A, 2586 RV Scheveningen, The Hague, Netherlands. The restaurant is open Tuesdays to Saturday s from 11:30 am all the way to 11:30 pm. On Sunday's they're open from 3:00 in the afternoon to 11:30 in the evening.

District 5

Hungry for a quick meal and don't want to spend too much on food? Then District 5 can provide you with a hearty meal that's truly worth your money. The restaurant is known for serving 3 course meals under € 30. Although the meals tend to be basic with a selection from vegetarian, fish or meat, the food is no less than scrumptious.

District 5 is located at Van der Helstplein 17, 1073 AR Amsterdam, Netherlands. They are open during Mondays, Wednesdays, and Sundays from 6 pm 10.30 pm.

Bacco Perbacco Cucina Italiana Restaurant

Bacco Perbacco Cucina Italiana Restaurant is one of the top restaurants in southern areas of the The Hague. They serve authentic Italian cuisine here and it's something that the Italians can truly be proud of. The chefs sometimes enveils part of their creativity when they whip up something new and out of the ordinary. Their selection of wines perfectly matches the dishes being served there. The restaurant is easily accessible; you can take the Randstadrail from pretty much anywhere in The Hague and you will pass by the place along the way.

Bacco Perbacco Cucina Italiana Restaurant is located at Van Speijkstraat 246 | 2518 DK, The Hague, The Netherlands.

New King

This is the place where you can satisfy your craving for Chinese food. Well, the menu leans toward Mandarin Chinese, which can prove to be a bit of an adventure for your taste buds. Don't miss out on their specialty – roast duck. Their wine list may not be that great and the service may not always be the best you can find in town but the food is worth all the trouble.

New King is located at Zeedijk 115-117, 1012 AV Amsterdam, Netherlands. They are open daily from 11 in the morning to 10.30 in the evening.

Take Thai

The minimalist design of the décor suits the overall atmosphere you'll get in Take Thai. The food of course is classic Thai cuisine; well, the name should be enough to hint at that. The food is spicy and rich – not to mention quite addictive (that is if you're into spicy food). The good news is that the prices are budget friendly even if the restaurant is located in a rather upscale part of town.

Take Thai is located at Utrechtsestraat 87, 1017 VK Amsterdam, Netherlands. They're open on Mondays and Tuesdays from 6 to 10 pm. On Wednesdays to Sundays they are open from noon to 3 pm.

Chapter 6: Top Shopping Sites In The Netherlands

Shopping In Amsterdam

The capital city of Amsterdam has a lot to offer to tourist shoppers. The area of Amsterdam-Zuid is a haven for tourists who prefer luxury brands. From Leidseplein to P.C. Hooftstraat, visitors can find the most luxurious and exclusive shops. For those tourists who prefer exclusive and original boutiques, the 9 Straatjes is the perfect shopping place. These small streets of fashion boutiques are located between the Singel, Prinsengracht, Leidsestraat, and Rozengracht.

Aside from restaurants, architecture, and museums, Amsterdam has a lot of fashion talent. The city center offers huge shopping streets such as Nieuwendijk, Kalverstraat, and Leidsestraat. World-renowned fashion chains and other shops are to be found in the city center. Smaller designer shops are in Jordaan. Chic shopping streets like Beethovenstraat, Van Baerlestraat, and PC Hooftstraat which offer international brands are in Zuid. The district of De Wallen has Oudezijds Achterburgwal offers various special designer shops.

Shopping In Rotterdam

A lot of unique shops are found in Rotterdam. Tourists, who want to buy something ordinary, will be surprised at what the city can offer. Groos is a concept store which sells Rotterdam-made products only while ANSH caters to women who prefer exclusive brands. Tourists who prefer talented yet new designers can check out Nen. Men and women can surely find affordable vintage and timeless pieces. Women who love to shop for shoes will surely find shopping at Betsy Palmer a delightful experience.

C. Cruden is a store which sells special denim products while Ginza sells exclusive sneakers. Tourists who want to shop for accessories, tutus, coats, trench coats, and sweatshirts can buy exclusive brands at Objet Trouve. They can find exclusive but affordable items at Louen. Those tourists who enjoy a Rock 'n Roll lifestyle will surely finf something retro at Very Cherry. A concept store like Gussie & Doortje sells great food, art, interior items, and vintage apparel. The street of Beurstraverse has big stores which sell popular brands while the districts of Pannekoekstraat & Nieuwemarkt offer special design, retro, and Bohemian shops.

The street of Witte de Withstraat offers avant-garde fashion boutiques, cafes, and galleries. For the young and trendy, the district of De Meent has single-brand shops and concept stores. For shoes, jewelry, and fashion shops, tourists can also head to the Nieuwe Binnenweg and Oude Binnenweg. The fashion district of Rotterdam can be found in Kruiskade and Van Oldebarneveltstraat. Lastly, the district of Oude Noorden is full of creative business people and young designers.

Shopping In The Hague

The city center of The Hague offers popular brands in the streets of Grote Marktstraat, Haagse Bluf, and Spuistraat. Sophisticated brands are found in Frederiksstraat, Denneweg, and Plaats square. Exclusive shoe boutiques and haute couture are in Molenstraat and Hoogstraat. The street of Frederik Hendriklaan has everything for each shopper. It offers food, home decors, gifts, and fashion items. Tourists who prefer unique items troop to this street.

Shopping In Maastricht

A lot of markets are found in the city of Maastricht. Tourists can find a lot fresh food, antique furniture, and other wares. Near the city hall and the mansions, visitors can check out the Maastricht Market which is open on Wednesdays and Fridays only. Fresh produce, food, cosmetics, clothes, flowers, and plants are sold in various stalls. On Wednesdays, there are about 200 stalls offering various products to consumers. On Fridays, additional stalls are opened for the fish market. The Stationsstraat, on the other hand, sells organic products on Thursdays. On Saturdays, it is transformed into a flea market.

Shopping In Utrecht

The city of Utrecht is a perfect place for shopping. The city center's Lijnmarkt has fashion and shoe stores. The Oude Gracht, on the other hand, offers different jewelry and special fashion shops. The shopping streets of Domstraat and Korte Jansstraat are popular to tourists who prefer specialty shops. Visitors who want to shop in exclusive, small boutiques can head to the historical streets of Korte Minrebroederstraat and Schoutenstraat.

Like the city of Maastricht, Utrecht also has markets. In fact, the city center hosts 3 large markets. The fabric market is found in Breedstraat, which is recognized as the oldest and largest fabric market in the Netherlands. it is open on Saturdays until 1pm. The flower market is open every Saturday in Janskerkhof and in the streets of Bakkerbrug and Oude Gracht. Lastly, the general market is open every Wednesday, Friday, and Saturday at Vredenburg.

Chapter 7: Recommended Malls and Shopping Centers for First Timers

The Netherlands is no stranger to the insanity of shopping madness. Fashion centers and chic shops literally dot the country. Even if you walk around in street markets you'll be surprised to find a lot of signature items on sale – at a very cheap price too! The following provides some important details about the different malls and shopping centers in the country.

Kalverstraat

Kalverstraat is probably the busiest shopping hub in Amsterdam. This shopping zone is more than just your ordinary pedestrian pathway. This narrow street is lined with snack bars, restaurants, bookstores, shoe stores, fashion boutiques, music stores, clothing and apparel shops, and much more. The street prices fluctuate and expect some items to be dirt cheap even though you're holding a signature brand and at times certain articles are just as expensive as the ones sold in department stores. Kalverstraat is the street that runs from Muntplein and Dam Square. It's pretty easy to find – just follow the crowd.

Kalvertoren

Kalvertoren is one of the more popular malls on Kalverstraat. If you find street prices of your favorite items to be a bit too much then you can walk into this mall and get something brand spanking new for the same price. People usually come through here if not for the deli treat then for the clothes. They also have a paint center here as well as a deli center where you can treat yourself some snacks. This mall also has more than 30 brand name stores which include Hugo Boss, Hema, and H&M among many others. Kalvertoren is right on the Kalverstraat; and it will be hard to miss this 3 storey building.

Albert Cuyp Market

Albert Cuyp Market is actually one of the biggest open air markets in the area. Some claim that it is actually one of the biggest markets in all of Europe. If you're looking for bargain priced goods then this is one of the go to places in the Netherlands. This market has pretty much everything from seafood to clothing and clothing accessories. If you need to sample some of the best cheeses in town then look for the row of cheese vendors. You may also try some of the delicacies on sale such as stroopwafels and kroketten. You'll find this enormous open air market at Albert Cuypstraat, Amsterdam, Netherlands.

Magna Plaza

Would you believe that this ornately designed shopping center was once a post office? Yes, the building that now houses Magna Plaza was the heart of the city's postal service beginning in 1899. The mall today has since become a family friendly center. There are shops that sell items for your home interior needs. Among the stalls and boutiques spread out on its four floors, you'll also find a toy center that will always be a big hit with the younger children. You can find the Magna Plaza at Nieuwezijds Voorburgwal 182, Amsterdam, 1012 SJ. They're open 11 am to 7 pm on Mondays, 10 am to 7 pm on Tuesdays to Saturdays, 10 am to 9 pm on Thursdays, and noon to 7 pm on Sundays.

Spiegelkwartier

If you're a big fan or a collector of antiques then this is the shopping center for you. If you fancy some contemporary paintings or sculptures then this is also the place for you. Spiegelkwartier is located in the more affluent part of the city. You'll find lots of high quality porcelain and the very best of decorative goods anywhere. If you have enough money to splurge on souvenirs then this is where you will find the most memorable mementos of your journey to the Netherlands. You'll find this one of a kind shopping district in Nieuwe Spiegelstraat, Amsterdam.

PC Hooftstraat

PC Hooftstraat is another really popular street for shoppers in the Netherlands. It's actually the place in town where fashion trendy people would prefer to visit. You don't actually have to buy anything. Window shopping is actually quite a trend here. However, if you have splurging money then why not treat yourself to a fashionable new coat, handbag, or at least the coolest pair of shades on earth? A bit of a warning though is that the prices here are ridiculously high. Well, that shouldn't be a surprise with labels such as Ralph Lauren, Louis Vuitton, Hugo Boss, Chanel, Gucci, Mulberry, Lacoste, and lots of other signature brands.

Haarlemmerstraat & Haarlemmerdijk

Do you want to have a fun satisfying shopping day without draining all your shopping funds? Then head walk right ahead to Haarlemmerstraat & Haarlemmerdijk. It's a shopping district that's slightly off the trodden path, so to speak. You'll find a mix of pretty much everything here. There are stores that sell kitchen gadgets that you usually find in the home TV shopping network. There are stalls that sell fashionable items and signature clothing. You will also find a plethora of specialty shops lining the street. If ever you feel famished then there are lots of grab and go stalls where you can snag a snack and go on with your shopping. You can even cap the day with a fun movie in the oldest cinema in town, which they aptly call The Movies (no pun intended right there).

Maison de Bonneterie

If you're more into distinct luxury shopping and would love to separate yourself from the common crowd then the Maison de Bonneterie is where you ought to be. You won't usually see a crowd of people here simply because only the elect of the elect ever dare to set foot here. The elegance of the building's exterior bespeaks of upscale wonders for you to behold inside. The items on sale here are reserved only for those who believe that money is no object. Luxury items from fashion labels such as Ralph Lauren, Scotch & Soda, Hugo Boss, Marc Jacobs, and G-Star are at your fingertips right here.

Lange Voorhout

This is one of the main shopping streets in The Hague. One of the main attractions here is the weekly book market, which is usually a huge hit. You'll also notice that the street is line with antique shop after antique shop. This street is also considered an antique lover's paradise. Another highlight is the market that sells all organic produce, which is located on

Grote Kerk Street. The market day usually starts at 11 in the morning and everyone closes shop at 7 in the evening.

Noordeinde and Denneweg

Tourists looking for haute couture shops in The Hague should stop by Noordeinde and Denneweg. These two streets are parallel to one another right at the Binnenhof government center. You'll also find a lot of antique stores and boutique shops on these shopping streets. They're also lined with cafes in case shoppers get hungry.

American Book Center

This book center specially caters to the English reading public. That basically includes expatriots who now reside in The Netherlands. Of course, a lot of the residents come here too just to get some of their latest collections. You'll find a lot of popular and not that well known titles. They sell both brand new and used books.

De Bijenkorf

Some people may think that they're walking into a museum when they visit De Bijenkorf. The building is fashioned after the manner of expressionist architecture, may come as a big surprise to some tourists. The brick and copper design are some of the key features of the building's design. The price range of the items on sale here range from mid-range to extremely pricey. Another highlight in this mall is the La Ruche Restaurant, which offers good food and stunning views of the city.

Maison de Bonneterie

If you're interested in shopping with the upper echelon then this is the place you need to be. It is said that the Queen Beatrix herself often comes here to do some of her personal shopping. The mall's structure is no less than regal with a glass dome that was affixed in 1913. As you may have guessed, this shopping center mainly caters to the upscale crowd. Here you will find some chic labels including Burberry, Hugo Boss, and Ralph Lauren among others.

De Passage

De Passage is noted as the oldest mall in The Hague. The building itself has been around since the 1800's. The building still fares pretty well and no one will even dare to call it an antique. You can say that this is where classic fashion meets with the hip and trendy, which is pretty much the oddly wonderful mix of the stores and shops you'll find here.

Alexandrium Shopping Center

Alexandrium Shopping Center is actually one of the largest shopping malls in Amsterdam. It houses the Woonmall, a cluster of megastores, and a huge shopping center. It houses more than 140 shops and boutiques, 16 mega retailers, electronics shops, and stalls. This shopping center opens at 9 am to 6 pm on Tuesdays to Saturdays. They open at 12 noon and close at 5 pm on Sundays. On Mondays they're open from 11 am to 6 pm.

Chapter 8: Top Beaches in The Netherlands

Aside from charming windmills and beautiful landscapes, The Netherlands is also famous for its beaches. Each year, a lot of tourists visit the beaches to enjoy the sea and the sand. The beaches of Zeeland, Flevoland, South Holland, North Holland, Groningen, and Friesland are top tourist attractions during the summer.

The beach of Zandvoort is found in the northern part of the country. Frequented by tourists, it is a nudist beach with a lot of restaurants, bars, and nature reserves. Visitors can enjoy kitesurfing, sailing, and windsurfing. The beach resort in Scheveningen is touted to be the country's best beach resort. It has a beautiful lighthouse, a harbor, an esplanade, and a pier. Guests can enjoy windsurfing. The beach also boasts of different restaurants, cafes, and bars.

Another popular beach for the family is Egmond aan Zee which also showcases a small museum and a fishing village. Tourists can find horses and wild foxes in the nearby dunes. The beach in Texel is frequented by adventurous and active visitors. Guests enjoy the mud walk and a bicycle ride around the area. The dune landscape also features a natural reserve.

Nudist Beaches In The Netherlands

Tourists become curious about the many naturist beaches in the country. Most of them haven't experienced going to a nudist beach because it is prohibited in their country of origin. In the Netherlands, nudism is permitted. Nudists have separate beaches or may have a part of the beach reserved for their use. The nudist beach in Callantsoog is considered the first nudist beach in the country. It was established in 1973? Nude sunbathers also have their own area on the beach. This beach can be accessed by train from Amsterdam. Tourists can take Intercity train to Schagen then take the Conexxion bus 152 to Callantsoog. They have to walk for 20 minutes to get to the beach.

Zandvoort beach has a place dedicated for nudists. It also offers drinks, meals, and snacks to them. Clothed patrons can have the other pavilions not assigned to nudists. Tourists can take train at Amsterdam CS if they want to go Zandvoort. They can get off at Zandvoort aan Zee then ride the Connexxion bus 81 to the beach. After alighting from the bus, they have to walk about 20 minutes to reach their destination. The beaches of Bloemendaal and Velsen share a nudist beach. Tourists can check out the other attractions surrounding the nudist area. This beach can be reached by taking the train at the Amsterdam Sloterdijk station. Travelers can then take the Connexxion Regioline 82 bus which will take them to IJmuiden aan Zee.

There's also a nudist beach at the northern part of The Netherlands. It is between Purmerend and Zaandam, near the Stootersplas lake. The Baaiegatstrand has been improved and was made safer and more spacious. This nudist beach can be accessed by taking the Amsterdam CS train. Tourists then ride the bus 92 to De Kunstgreep and walk for 25 minutes to the beach. Lastly, nudists try nude relaxation, recreation, and sports at Flevo Natuur. It is not really a beach but nudists can ride horses, fish, surf, sail, swim, and sunbathe near Lake Nijkerkernauw in the Hulkesteinse forest. Tourists go to Flevo Natuur by taking the the Intercity train at Amsterdam CS to Almere Centrum. They take the Connexxion bus 160 to the Wielseweg bus stop the on walk for 15 minutes to the park.

Beach Hopping in The Netherlands

The coast of The Netherlands stretches from the Wadden Sea Islands to Zeeland. Beach bars, family beaches, surfer hangouts, and narurist areas have their own places in the region. The water can be cold and brown unlike the crystal clear blue and warm waters of the Mediterranean. Temperatures can range from 2 degrees Celsius to 20 degrees Celsius. Surf schools recommend using a wetsuit in order to deal with the cold waters. The beach waters are analyzed regularly by the infrastructure ministry during the summer season to check the water quality.

If the beach has a blue flag, it means that it is safe and clean. Not all beaches in the country has a blue flag because some beaches have sewage problems. Each year, millions of visitors go the Dutch beaches. German tourists are the top visitors. Guests can explore the flora and fauna, bike to the dunes, try out the local cuisine, and take yoga, beach football, and surf lessons. A total of 350 summer pavilions are prepared to welcome tourists during the summer season.

Travelers who take a Dutch beach holiday can opt for bed & breakfat, campsite, holiday park, or a hotel experience. Beach huts are also available in warmer months. During the winter season, tourists can kite surf, jog, or walk around the beach.

Chapter 9: Recommended Beaches for First Timers

The Netherlands is home to some of the best beaches in the world. The beaches are definitely great idyllic places where visitors can just stretch out and enjoy the beautiful scenery. Other than that, you can just frolick in the sands or dip the beautiful ocean water.

Note that the Dutch are quite a crafty folk especially in Amsterdam where no one would expect to have any beaches whatsoever. Some of the beaches in our list are actually man-made and artificial. You can consider them to be both a beach and a party place.

Scheveningen

Scheveningen is arguably the best beach you can find in the Netherlands. Of course some of these beaches there are better than others. However, all of the beaches in the country have something unique to offer. Some of the key features of this beach and its immediate area include a rather stunning lighthouse, a pier, and an esplanade.

Due to its popularity, a lot of bars, restaurants, and cafes have been established at the beach area. A local casino was also established, which further diversifies the offerings of this beach. The night comes alive with beach parties attended by locals as well as foreign tourists. If you're not the partying type then you can also go shopping or perhaps see how well you fare in bowling. Scheveningen is one of the districts of The Hague. It is popular destination for kiteboarders and windsurfers.

Egmond aan Zee

Ask any of the locals about the great beaches in Netherlands and they will most likely include Egmond aan Zee in their specific list. If you're in the country for some quality family time, then you better bring everyone here. The nearby fishing village holds many interesting things as well. That includes a small museum and the town's own lighthouse. You can also bring the kids along to see some wildlife at the dunes.

There are lots of bed and breakfast places here so finding a room for the night isn't going to be an issue. Other than the usual beach frolicking and sun worshipping, there are lots of family friendly activities that everyone can enjoy. Egmond aan Zee is 9 kilometers west of Alkmaar on the northern coast of North Holland.

Texel

Texel is one of beaches in Holland that get the most sunshine. If you're looking for a place to get a good tan then this place is a pretty good candidate. The island is a place for a lot of outdoor fun. You will find a lot of folks riding bikes or hiking around the dunes. Do take care not to disturb the natural surroundings since much of the area is a protected natural reserve. The northern area of the island is also worth visiting. The lighthouse there is quite iconic too.

The white sand beaches here are quite broad. That means you don't have to worry even if a huge crowd gathers on the sands because you'll always have some beach space to claim as your own. If riding bicycles isn't your thing then try horseback riding to add a little thrill to your Texel adventure.

Strand Zuid

Strand Zuid is a big surprise to anyone visiting Amsterdam. You wouldn't think there are beaches here but yes there are. Strand Zuid is actually a man made beach that stretches to about 2,000 square miles. This beach is the place for the partying type where things are trendy and absolutely fashionable. There are lots of upscale pubs and the bars here serve customers with a lot of gusto. Don't let the looks of the place scare you off – it's not going to kill your vacation budget. It's the place where you can hang out and meet the local crowd.

Kijkduin

Kijkduin is the second most popular beach resort in The Hague. Kijkduin is located at the North Sea and is actually a seaside resort in South Holland. Visitors will enjoy the long stretch of sand and sea, which makes the place quite popular.

The place actually offers more than just the proverbial sun, sand, and sea. The nearby town has lots of boutiques, jewelry stores, and fahion centers. You may also shop for souvenirs along the way too. Finding a place to eat isn't going to be an issue as well since there are plenty of restaurants that serve, a fusion of Italian, Mexican, French, and the local Dutch cuisine.

Strand Blijburg

Strand Blijburg is another man-made beach in Amsterdam. It is also a popular getaway from the busy city life. It's actually one of the few artificially constructed beaches here where you can go out and swim. The beach is actually part of the bar and restaurant that also bears the same name. Enjoy great food, lavish drinks, camp fires, and evening music.

Getting to Strand Blijburg is really easy. You just need to hop on tram 26 from the city's central station. You get off at Ruisrietstraat and take a short stroll. Alternatively, you can take Bus 66 which actually stops there right in front of the beach.

Strand West

Strand West is the local beach in Amsterdam where the younger folks gather and meet. It's pretty huge, which covers 20,000 square meters. Visitors here are treated to a lovely panoramic view of the nearby waters. This man-made beach is quite close to the city center. A good tip is for you to rent a bike so you won't have to rely on the bus to get home. That means you can stay on the beach and party all night even after the last bus going back to the suburbs has gone. It's only a 10 minute bike ride so you don't really have to cover a lot of distance.

Strand Ijburg

Strand Ijburg carries with it a peculiar hippie vibe that is rather welcoming for the entire family. There are beach restaurants that offer a wide range of delicacies, music, and drinks for the entire family. The big advantage of this beach of Strand Zuid and Strand West is the fact that you can actually swim in the nearby waters. If swimming is your thing then you can also try some of the watersports. If you're new to kitesurfing and such, the shop owners can also offer to teach you the basics for a reasonable price. To get to Strand Ijburg, hop on a tram at line 26.

Chapter 10: Arts and Culture in The Netherlands

The Netherlands is a densely-populated, small country which is located in Western Europe. It is adjacent to Germany, Belgium, and the North Sea. The cities of Rotterdam, The Hague, and Amsterdam are the most important and largest cities. The country name means Low Country because of its flat and low geography. It is the primary exporter of agriculture and food products to the United States of America. The country is governed as a constitutional monarchy and parliamentary democracy. It is regarded as a liberal nation which legalized euthanasia, prostitution, and abortion. Its drug policy is considered as progressive. Same-sex marriage was legalizes in 2001.

In the world of arts, The Netherlands has world-renowned painters like Jacob van Ruysdael, Jan Steen, Johannes Vermeer, and Rembrandt van Rijn in the 17th century. From the 19th to the 20th century, it has produced painters like Piet Mondriaan and Vincent van Gogh. Spinoza and Erasmus are popular philosophers. During its Golden Age, the country has produced famous writers like P.C. Hooft and Joosr van den Vondel. In the 29th century, The Netherlands had writers like Willem Frederik Hermans, Gerard Reve, Cees Nooteboom, Hella S. Haasse, Simon Vestdijk, Jan Wolkers, and Harry Mulisch. The Diary of Anne Frank has been translated to different languages. Dutch building replicas are found in Nagasaki, Japan and Shenyang, China. Tourists visit The Netherlands because of its cannabis, Delftware pottery, cheese, wooden shoes, tulips, and windmills.

Social behavior is dictated by the Dutch etiquette code. Books have been written about the Dutch etiquette. Some of these customs are still practiced in some Dutch regions. Furthermore, European etiquette is also practiced in the country. The Dutch people are modern, individualistic, and egalitarian. They see themselves as self-reliant, independent, and modest. Ability is valued over dependency. The Dutch don't like non-essential things. In fact, ostentatious behavior is frowned upon. Spending a lot of money in public is a show-off and is even considered a vice.

A luxurious lifestyle is considered a waste of money. The Dutch people are proud of their international involvement in various affairs. They are proud of their rich art history and cultural heritage. In terms of manners, they are blunt, informal, and have a no-nonsense attitude. They also follow basic behaviors. Other cultures consider the Dutch as patronizing and impersonal. Some people even consider them rude. Their cuisine is shape by farming ang fishing practices. By tradition, their cuisine is straightforward and simple with little meat and a lot of vegetables. Bread with toppings is considered breakfast and lunch while meat, potatoes, and vegetables are served at dinner. Their diet is rich in fat and carbohydrates which reflect the needs of laborers in the country. In the 20th century, this diet became more modern. Most Dutch cities now offer international cuisines.

Music traditions are aplenty in The Netherlands. Traditional music consists of simple rhythm and melody with straightforward refrains and couplets. Songs are often about loneliness, death, and love. Traditional musical instruments include the barrel organ and accordion. Andre Hazes, Frans Bauer, and Jan Smith are known as traditional musicians. Modern pop and rock music started in the 1960s and were influenced by music from the USA and Britain. Dutch bands like Focus, Golden Earring, and Shocking Blue enjoyed monumental success not only in the country but in international fronts as well. By the 1980s, songs were written in the Dutch language. Currently, pop music enjoys air waves in both languages. Symphonic Metal bands Within Temptation and Epica with pop/jazz singer Caro Emerald are enjoying international success.

Many Dutch films enjoyed international recognition and distribution. The Fourth Man, Spetters, Soldier of Orange, and Turkish Delight were some of the internationally known films of director Paul Verhoeven. He also directed Hollywood movies like Basic Instinct and RoboCop. In 2006, he went back to directing Dutch films through Black Book. Fons Rademakers, Dick Maas, and Jan de Bont also became world-renowned Dutch film directors. Dutch actors like Derek de Lint, Jeroen Krabbe, Rutger Hauer, Carice van Houten, and Famke Janssen became successful internationally.

The world of sports has a huge following in The Netherlands. About 25% of the whole population is registered in various sports clubs. About 2/3 of the population has weekly sports activities. Football is very popular in the country, along with volleyball and field hockey. In terms of individual sports, golf, gymnastics, and tennis are very popular. The Netherlands has won a total of 266 medals from the Summer Olympics and 110 medals from the Winter Olympics. The women's hockey team is very successful in the World Cup while the country's baseball team has lorded over the European championship by winning 20 of the 32 games at stake. During the 2014 Winter Olympics, the speed skaters from The Netherlands have won 23 out of the 36 medals. Motorcycle racing is also popular in the country. The TT Assen Circuit has hosted the yearly Motorcycle World Championship since 1949.

The Netherlands is a country rich in culture and the arts. It's not surprising to find out that tourists flock to the country to experience first-hand what this European country has to offer. Aside from its rich culture, the country has a lot of tourist attractions, shopping and restaurant locations, as well as beautiful beaches for everyone. Tourists from around the world will surely find their The Netherlands experience truly a marvelous and enjoyable experience of a lifetime.

Chapter 11: Tourist Traps Netherlands

Even though the Netherlands is such a wonderful place to visit, there are a few tourist traps that you should avoid just like everywhere else. The following are some of the things that you should avoid on your trip to the country. Consider them as important tips to help you avoid trouble.

Tourist Trap #1 – Street Drugs

It's no secret that you can buy soft drugs in Amsterdam. The proper places to get them are in coffeeshops – yes, that's exactly what they're called. Some people may call them as coffee houses but of course they are referring to the same thing. As a bit of a warning, you should note that there are many unscrupulous people who will take a chance with tourists.

It doesn't take long before tourists here about foreigners getting duped into buying aspirin, parsley, or even sheep dung for premium drug prices. These people usually approach tourists and simple offers of "coke" or sometimes "hash." So, rule number one is to avoid street drugs and buy only from "coffeeshops." Oh yes, as an FYI, note that local laws prohibit the sale of drugs to minors (i.e. anyone younger than 18 years).

Tourist Trap #2 – Drop Off Your Luggage First (Basic Safety in Mind)

Some first time tourists in The Netherlands are overeager to see the sites in the country. There have been plenty of tourists, especially first timers, who drag their luggage around with them to museums, cafes, bars, and even to coffeeshops right after getting off the train. Remember that there are opportunistic thieves everywhere in the world and the Netherlands isn't an exception.

There have been many overeager tourists who carry everything with them from the airport or train and making a run for it to the nearest coffeeshop just to have their first sample of soft drugs. They end up stoned and become easy targets for thieves. This has happened a lot, so be warned.

The first thing you should do is to go to your hotel, book a room, drop off your luggage, and then go to wherever it is you intended to go. Another common mistake associated with new tourists is that they immediately flash their cash in public. Do that and you're immediately marked as a target. Some of the more experienced (not to mention wiser) tourists always have a money belt with them – practical tool right there. Always follow the usual precautions when visiting any foreign country: don't talk to junkies, beware of pickpockets, don't go into deserted or dark alleys, etc.

Tourist Trap #3 – Avoid So-Called "Erotic Museums"

There are plenty of museums in The Netherlands and erotic museums aren't part of the whole thing. The usual modus operandi is to lure tourists to come inside, look at the pictures, and sample the goods (i.e. special services) they have on sale. Well, if all you wanted to do is look at the "merchandise" then don't pay for it since there is plenty of that for free in the red light district. The operators of these outfits are just trying to dupe you into paying for something that is already free in the city.

Tourist Trap #4 – No Photographs Please (The Prostitute at the Window)

Taking a picture of the prostitute at the window in the Red Light District is a no-no. You can take a picture of pretty much everything else but not the scantily clad gorgeous women. You'll find yourself in a heap of trouble with the bouncers and may end up getting seriously injured. If you want a souvenir of the woman at the window then buy a postcard at the door. FYI – there is a Prostitute Information Center where you can get all the info with regard to proper conduct, behavior, and the rules that you should abide by while in the Red Light District.

Tourist Trap #4 – Don't Fall for the Free Cookie Treat

It has happened on more than a few occassions when a tourist is greeted by a lovely Dutch girl with a plate full of cookies. They will warmly greet you with a warm welcome to the country and even offer you a free treat. The tourist eats a cookie, gets drowsy, and finds himself robbed of pretty much everything. This happens just about anywhere – malls, cafes, discos, coffeeshops, and bars. Don't fall for it. Sometimes it's a pretty girl offering you a cookie, sometimes it's an innocent looking young boy, or a harmless granny.

Conclusion

Thank you again for purchasing this book!

I hope this book was able to help you to understand the culture and the arts in The Netherlands as well as inspire you take that well-deserved vacation to this country.

The next step is to book that flight to The Netherlands!

Finally, if you enjoyed this book, please take the time to share your thoughts and post a review on Amazon. We do our best to reach out to readers and provide the best value we can. Your positive review will help us achieve that. It'd be greatly appreciated!

Thank you and good luck!

Check Out My Other Books

Below you'll find some of my other popular books that are popular on Amazon and Kindle as well. Simply click on the links below to check them out. Alternatively, you can visit my author page on Amazon to see other work done by me.

The Best of England For Tourists

http://amzn.to/1rv7RVZ

The Best of Beautiful Greece For Tourists

http://amzn.to/1u9Xclw

The Best of Italy For Tourists

http://amzn.to/1kNIqYm

The Best of Spain For Tourists

http://amzn.to/1zHGGII

The Best of Beautiful Germany For Tourists

http://amzn.to/V4SoiT

The Best of Brazil For Tourists

http://amzn.to/1sCoSdT

The Best of Beautiful France For Tourists

http://amzn.to/1yD7yal

If the links do not work, for whatever reason, you can simply search for these titles on the Amazon website to find them.

20371556R00033

Made in the USA
San Bernardino, CA
08 April 2015